Between the Strings Vol. I

To my garden that's not so secret

Author's note

Letting you into my diaries again. I must be insane.

Hope you can take something from the journey of my preteen + teen years. xx

TWs: This book contains material relating to

food struggles, memory loss, childhood trauma, anxiety, depression, addiction, verbal abuse, physical abuse, substance abuse, sexual assault, self-harm, suicide, and possibly more

~ TABLE OF CONTENTS ~

Beginning
~ INTRODUCTIONS
~ TWELVE
~ THE DEMON AND THE DOLL
~ DAYS
~ AND WHEN
~ I'M THE DUNGEON, NOT THE PRINCESS LOCKED INSIDE
~ SWEET KISSES
~ A FRIEND
~ OPENING SCENE
~ BYE BYE BARBARA
~ HOW I "BECAME GOD"
~ A FEW THINGS I LEARNED
~ DOMINOES
~ FRAGILITY
~ BLUE OR BROWN

Middle
~ I DON'T WORK ANYMORE
~ XANAX
~ THERE'S A SONG ABOUT THIS WORD
~ THE SAINTS
~ LAUGHING FLOWERS
~ POM-POMS
~ SCARS
~ RED WIRE
~ FALSE ALARM
~ DRUMS AND OTHERS
~ ~~GREEN BEA~~R
~ FAMILY HEIRLOOM(S)
~ ~~HEAVY~~WEIGHT
~ CHAMBER MUSIC
~ THE MANY TALENTS OF GLASS
~ BLONDIE
~ BEG SHOULDERS KNEES AND TOES
~ SHE'S UGLY

~ IT'S NOT MY PARTY AND I'LL CRY IF I WANT TO
~ I THINK I KNOW
~ FAIRYTALE
~ FAIRYTALE II
~ CHAMPAIN PROBLEMS
~ FEIGNED AFFAIRS
~ HE WISHED IT WORKED
~ THE MIND OF HISTORY
~ WHAT TIME SHOULD DO
~ *shrugs*
~ NEW OPTIONS IN THE TOY CHEST
~ THE THING ABOUT SUNSETS
~ PLEASE DON'T LEAVE ME
~ IT'S NOT AS CUTE AS IT SOUNDS
~ SLEEPY NOT SLEEPY
~ CLEAN UP TIME
~ DRUG OF CHOICE
~ SACRIFICE
~ SAVIOR
~ IF ONLY
~ EMPTY ~~BOTTLES~~
~ JAILBIRD
~ STROBE LIGHTS
~ MIDAS
~ BABY'S BLUE
~ IF I WERE HONEST FOR A SECOND, ~~BUT I RAN OUT OF TIME~~
~ INSECURITIES
~ STOP CALLING ME THAT
~ IT'S NOT SPIDERS
~ SUNNY
~ CUT MYSELF "SHAVING"
~ GALLOWS
~ ~~UN~~NATURAL DISASTERS
~ PILL POPPER
~ COLD WATER
~ SHE HAD YOUR BABY
~ AND I DIDN'T EVEN NEED ADVERTISING
~ WHAT I LEARNED TO DO WITH FEELINGS

~ A FUN FACT ABOUT THE DEVIL
~ KIDDIE DRAWINGS
~ MIDNIGHT
~ A SAD GIRL MOMENT

~ TIED UP
~ TIED UP II
~ MATH

Beginning

~ **Beginning playlist** ~

A Beautiful Spring Day - From "101 Dalmatians"/Score Version ~ George Bruns
A Dream Is a Wish Your Heart Makes - From "Cinderella"/Soundtrack Version ~ Ilene Woods, Mice Chorus
When You Wish Upon a Star ~ Cliff Edwards, Disney Studio Chorus
Tornado Warning ~ Harald Kloser
Luck Dries Up ~ Mark Isham
The Final Arrow ~ Marc Streitenfeld
A World Destroyed ~ Fernando Velázquez
Goodbyes ~ Harald Kloser, Thomas Wander
The Only Way is Down ~ Thomas Newman
Peeta's Broadcast ~ James Newton Howard
Victory ~ James Newton Howard
Richat ~ Mark Petrie
Deep Shadow ~ T.T.L.
Vigil ~ Bill Conti, David Duke
Main Title (Alice in Wonderland) ~ The Jud Conlon Chorus
Trapdoor ~ Twenty One Pilots
The Others ~ Rendez Vous
Take Me Away ~ New Medicine
Someone's Waiting for You - From "The Rescuers"/Soundtrack Version ~ Shelby Flint

INTRODUCTIONS

Où est ton papa?
Dis-moi, où est ton papa?
Sans même devoir lui parler
Il sait ce qu'il ne va pas

"Lift your arms."
She could feel the silver beginning to line her eyes.
Where was he? Where were they?
Wordlessly, she allowed them to rise from her sides. Not one cry,
not one whimper. Both, along with other things, had already been choked
out of her. The smooth satin of her dress slip greatly contradicted the temper
of her environment. The feel of the silky material against her skin was enough
to nearly send her careening over the edge. The actual dress fell over it
with a flourish.
White. Of course it was.
No one would tell her his name, but when the lesser shadows—hardly more
than suppressed winds, silhouettes in the surrounding dark—whispered
about him, she'd hear words such as, "chaos, fear, anger."
Maybe it was one of those.
He *would* make sure it was white. Evidence of his immoral sense of humor.
But she considered it a small mercy that he hadn't made it purple.
It was a pretty dress, too.
More proof.
They may not have spoken much yet, but he knew well enough to know that
she hadn't wanted to be thrown into a pretty dress.
Not when her world was so ugly and she was its mirror image.

Her socks and shoes were shoved onto her feet with all the gentleness of a thunderclap, yet being mere minutes away from seeing
Shadow had hardly allowed the fact to register.
They had yet to be properly introduced, is how it was put to her.
The blood that stained her most recent memories begged to differ.
Blood on a tiny blade, and it was all her fault, all her fault—
She blinked, and a hand was in hers, leading her toward the door.
All the hands were cold here. Hers soon would be too.
From far away, with every step of her ivory-clad feet, she could hear the words of a song, in a language not her own, but words her heart
had understood since the beginning.
One step.
Où est ton papa?
Another.
Dis-moi, où est ton papa?
Another.
Sans même devoir lui parler
Il sait ce qu'il ne va pas
Over and over, the words turned as her feet made their way along the icy stone beneath them. Not unlike her, they seemed to be looking for something.
But I suppose they're gone.
The shadow's hand (no one had given her *their* name either, so she'd decided they were shadows, and he was Shadow) gripped the handle to turn it and walk the girl to her doom, but all the girl saw was the
pale, corpse-like hand. It was the one thing that had gripped her attention throughout the entire ordeal. She nearly fainted.
The repercussions for that would be monstrous, indeed;
she swiftly shoved the feeling down and averted her eyes
from the sight.

(Poor thing. She was learning already.)
The shadow opened the door and led her down the hallway.

Où est ton papa?
Dis-moi, où est ton papa?
Sans même devoir lui parler
Il sait ce qu'il ne va pas

TWELVE

I suppose the clouds should've been a warning.
I'd never seen them look like that.
Green. Like the color of those imaginary monsters under your bed
when you were a child. Stacked on top of each other,
one haphazardly on top of the next, like too many lies trying
to cover the truth.
Lightning strikes shot through the sky as if its hand had never held a gun,
blinding white bullets ricocheting off its walls.

It was orientation. Seventh grade. Everyone returned in that normal, bright-eyed, bushy-tailed way that kids do after summer. Freshly tanned, a few with new hair colors or highlights at least, dreading the impending schoolwork but not dreading finally being with each other every day once again. Chatter about vacations and new hobbies bounced from room to room through propped classroom doors. Everyone roamed in and out, the air of a new year hanging over our heads like a crystal chandelier.

~~~~~

It's the end of orientation. My homeroom class. This room in particular had these floor-to-ceiling glass walls on one side.
Which was unfortunate, because it gave me a perfect view of the storm.
Gave the storm a perfect view of me.

Its voice slithered underneath the glass and snaked around the desks,
dampening the words from the teacher's mouth as if a pillow
was being held to his face.
As his words were being pulled under by the current,
one reaching hand outstretched toward the sky for salvation,
the storm's were rising to the surface.
And I didn't listen. I didn't know I was supposed to.

THE DEMON AND THE DOLL

One of them has decided to show his face and play.
But this doll is tired and wants to enjoy Sleep
while she's got him in her grasp.
(It was a *chase,* indeed.)
So she looks this *thing* dead in the eyes… maybe for a moment too long,
but she can't figure out whether or not he's real—
if he's a danger or a hallucination birthed from the grave of her mind.
He looks hideous. His face—all of the features too large, as if she was staring
at them from underneath a magnifying glass—is the Abyss given form, a
black that stands stark against the *night* and has no end.
Save for the holes of yellow. A sickly neon, too bright.
She doesn't care.
She rolls over.
(And dares to utter a prayer from her heart to His ears,
hoping He doesn't find her voice strange.)

Let him play elsewhere tonight.

DAYS

Day 2,554.
You'd think he'd have used the time to get creative.
Although I don't suppose I would bother getting creative
with a corpse, either.
His eyes rake over me slowly, dragging as if they've just gotten out of bed,
and it's still too quick. I hate this look, mostly because
it's the one I've been getting lately every time he sees me,
and I figured out what it said the second time around.
It starts at my feet, and by the time he makes it to my face, he's smirking,
just barely—that's intentional, too—one side of his mouth
quirked up in a faint smile.
Because he notices I've lost weight.

AND WHEN

I was left to grieve all the ways I used to believe
I was actually doing *something*.
But so many hands brushing the fingertips
of Death's surrounded me...
the cold of them numbed me to my tiny fragile bones.

Words that weren't stones,
but instead the hills I was dying on.
I didn't know, I'm sorry. I didn't mean to be a noose.
That's no excuse, the red on his wrists told me.
And I believed it was right.

And when the darkness fell and wrapped its hands around my throat,
I learned what it meant for things to go bump in the night.

I'M THE DUNGEON, NOT THE PRINCESS LOCKED INSIDE

That place, where they lock you up and throw away the key.
That place is me, haven't you heard?
I've been hearing these words ever since I was a girl—
unspoken words are very loud, you see, especially to ears like mine.

Ever since I was younger, I've only ever wanted to be
a saving grace kind of key,
the one you slip from the waist of the guard outside the cell
when all hope was lost moments before.
Unknown in all ways to me,
when, where,
in every way except why,
along the way, I became the cell itself.
The feeling is a forever kind of falling, little to no chance
of smooth landing.
I'm locked in me, too.

SWEET KISSES

I remember little before I started falling.
One vague memory—so far in the back of my mind
that my feet ache from traveling to find it—comes to mind.
Sweet kisses. *Innocent.*
I almost laugh at the word as I think it.
The girl on the other end of those lips died a long time ago,
at least mostly.
When she finally tripped over the devil's foot
and fell where he wanted her,
she didn't get to take those kisses with her.
The innocence, either.

A FRIEND

He'd left her next to the pink dollhouse.
Sprawled, at all the wrong angles, discarded on the floor like garbage.
That wasn't her.
Whoever this was—
What wasn't bloodied was broken, what wasn't broken was... gone.
The right hand is missing two fingers.
I'm going to vomit.
The left arm is bent inward, pointing toward a gruesome bloodstain spread across the broken-down floorboards. Both of the legs look...
I empty the contents of my stomach onto the floor.
I look where the face is supposed to be but clearly isn't.
Just a swollen, disfigured mess left in its place. But I had to walk around to see all of it because the neck was twisted away from me.
I sink to my knees and slowly turn her face toward me with one of my hands.
I leave it there for I don't know how long. At some point I took both hands and cradled her head in my lap. At another, one of my thumbs rubbed soothing circles along her cheek;
I'm not sure why. The damage was done.

~~~~~

Have I been here for three days, too?

I don't know how long I've been down here.

I leave about two lifetimes later.

OPENING SCENE

You know those scenes in movies when trouble's
about to overtake the town?
A single streetlight hums a slow song to pass the remaining hours.
Its eyes start to try and blink away the abnormal sleep ready to
overcome it and the rest of its friends.
To no avail. A too-fast-too-slow series of desperate blinks later,
and it cuts. Then another—his best friend.
Soon, the entire street is shrouded in darkness.
The camera pans to another part of town, the commonplace area, probably
the diner or something like that. The sign showcasing its name blinks
relentlessly, hell-bent on winning the fight the streetlights lost, but it's no use.
It shudders to black,
and the people inside stop cold, in the middle of their idle,
unimportant conversations.
Cue the dramatic montage of various areas of the city, welcoming gloom into
their humble abodes for who knows how long,
until the city gets itself back in order.
And then you have the camera panning to the reason it all went dark.
You feel him before you see him.

I am the forsaken town. And the first streetlight just went out.

BYE BYE BARBARA

I turned to my right to wave goodbye.
She still looked exactly the same; she always did.
Brilliant blue eyes, this vibrant blue you can't mimic, really.
There's always light in the corners of them.
Lips so pink they look like they just got kissed goodnight.
Not even a visible pore on her face.
Perfect, the textbook definition.
I had to get away from her.

HOW I "BECAME GOD"

All it took was one convincing lie,
one bullet to the brain of my innocence.

The dolls weren't plastic anymore,
and there were new games to play.

A FEW THINGS I LEARNED

I wasn't lying when I said they didn't consume me.
But they did… teach me a few things.
What'd you expect—was I supposed to sit idle
while they covered me?
Not likely. If I *was* going to die, I was at least going to do so
with a few tricks up my sleeve.

Classes took place in the midst of every toss and turn.
The first thing I learned was how to hide—hiding without hiding. Standing unseen in the middle of a room. And they told me there was no better place to learn that than a graveyard.

This stupid graveyard.
One of our unspoken stipulations, it feels like; they drag me here almost every day, and I'm forced to listen to them prattle on and on and on.
Today, I'm the perfect picture of composure that I don't feel. I cross my arms, fold my legs, and lean against one of the headstones. Spare a glance at the letters of the name, make out the first three letters, then look away. Reading it all would've just gutted me.
Their voices carry on the wind to where I'm standing, a ways away, and I suppress the urge to roll my eyes. One thing I can hardly stand about them is that there is always noise. Humming, singing, whispering, yelling. There's never any quiet. At this point, I've learned all their favorite songs that they've learned from the ghosts. They only sing them when we're here.
They really only sing one song back home.

DOMINOES

The first domino always falls the slowest.
Fools you into thinking the rest of them will fall that way, too.
That's why it bothers me how quickly it happened,
how fast it all fell in me.
I realized I was a house of cards and I hated that
because wouldn't you hate it if you thought you were stronger
and all it took was a little wind?

FRAGILITY

Like a lifted stone in otherwise smooth and solid ground,
like the loose floorboard in the house
that everyone's learned to avoid because if you step on it,
it makes too loud of a noise.
My mind had no two legs to stand on:
It was a glass set on the edge of a counter,
just waiting for the touch of a finger
to send it careening over the edge.

BLUE OR BROWN

Everybody's got their trail markers in the dark.
Mine was either a song
or a nice pair of blue or brown eyes,
whichever happened to infatuate me at the moment.

Middle

~ Middle playlist ~

Father's Song ~ Prince
Colors ~ Halsey
Colors pt. II ~ Halsey
Happy Little Pill ~ Troye Sivan
Habits (Stay High) - Hippie Sabotage Remix ~ Tove Lo, Hippie Sabotage
4 Morant (Better Luck Next Time) ~ Com Truise
Stuck ~ Dixie
Black Balloons ~ Ellise
Sleep Thru Ur Alarms ~ Lontalius
lovely (with Khalid) ~ Billie Eilish, Khalid
IM FINE ~ Royal & the Serpent
Polarize ~ Twenty One Pilots
I Think I'm In Love ~ Kat Dahlia
3 Strikes ~ Terror Jr
Gold ~ Kiiara
Hypnotic ~ Zella Day
On My Mind ~ Sofia Karlberg
Heathens ~ Twenty One Pilots
Make Me (Cry) - Marshmello Remix ~ Noah Cyrus, Labrinth, Marshmello
Rich Kids ~ Bea Miller
Super Rich Kids ~ Frank Ocean, Earl Sweatshirt
Sorrows ~ BLESSED
I Know You (with Matt Maeson) ~ Steinza, Matt Maeson

idfc - Tarro Remix ~ blackbear, Tarro
do re mi ~ blackbear
Blow Out ~ Radiohead
Wasted Summers ~ juju<3
Stay Together ~ Noah Cyrus
Bitter Taste ~ Billy Idol
Raise the Dead ~ Rachel Rabin
Moving Along ~ Knola

I DON'T WORK ANYMORE

I don't even know what it looked like outside today.
Did the sun bother to bless the sky with its presence,
or has it finally turned on the darkened girl beneath this roof,
who's becoming ripped at the corners?

XANAX

She ate 'em like candy.
And I bet if you asked her,
she'd tell you they were her favorite kind.
Her trembling hands steadily reached for the sunset bottle,
as if it wasn't always night here.
The sun left of its own accord. Not because of a bruised ego,
but because it cared. And couldn't watch.

THERE'S A SONG ABOUT THIS WORD

"Tomorrow."

That day always gets more than it deserves.

THE SAINTS

The saints here are starting to become familiar.
Only by faces. Never by names.
Every time we come here,
I can't help but stare at their arms. Their hands.
Something in me cringes
at their outstretched arms and wide open palms.
I want to ask Mary if she and the rest of the saints
are aware that that's a *sinner's* job.
I avert my eyes and move on—
let the saints live in their delusion.
Now I look at the One in the middle, and I don't turn my head.
Because I am the nail in His left hand.

LAUGHING FLOWERS

I'd bet every dollar I have that the world
wasn't always this bright.
Everything, so bright.
The flowers should turn their heads away
for the beauty they hold.
I glance at one before I can stop myself.
Its barely concealed smirk
prompts my eyes to find other places to look.

(Run an idle hand along one of the shelves in me,
and you'll come away with dust.)

POM-POMS

Couple girls in school said I was in the closet.
Only things in the closet were my skeletons,
and they knew it, too—but their deluded minds
were too wrapped up in condescension, pretension,
and their warped, sadistic intentions.
The shorter one—I guess she was upset
that I had his attention, and I didn't even need the cheer skirt.
The other one didn't like that with me,
he didn't even have to bend his head to get high.
Two dumb blonde brunettes
who pretended it was hard to guess
that the girl he was actually impressed with
had one foot over the cliff of dying inside.

Round and round the tears went behind my eyes
until they decided they had better things to cry about.

~~Bigger demons they'd try to drown out,~~
~~that walked on the waves of my sadness like dry land.~~
~~Distant voices reach beneath the currents,~~
~~their fingers telling me to *hold on*,~~
~~but the sinking body of my thoughts is saying *I can't*.~~

SCARS

His lips are soft. His lips are lies.
The scars on my back tell me as much—misshapen, crooked lines
that appear too much like frantic hands trying to point me
in the direction of home. And yet I still don't leave.
Instead, I allow these lips to plant featherlight kisses along the length
of my neck, each one a more horrible untruth than the last.
I know what you're thinking.
But I have to believe the lies he tells me.
I have to... his words are easier to swallow
than the food I can hardly keep down.
If I fight him now... I start over. I'm too weak to start over.
It's always been me and him, a likely-unlikely pairing,
match made in a place where the gates don't have pearls,
but broken bones instead.
Said to be the bones of wayward sons and daughters
who didn't listen to their scars.
I'm scared to go beyond these gates
to where I see the light in the distance.

RED WIRE

I'm not sure what your first thought is
when you wake up in the morning,
but when I open my eyes,
the first thing I wonder is if today will be the day.

Each heartbeat feels like a second of the clock counting down.
Each a reminder that my time is borrowed, not given.
Why would it be given?
I don't deserve it.

FALSE ALARM

The demons held my head to the water.
Their too-sharp fingernails dug into my scalp, pushing me forward...
to look.
A pathetic reflection stared back.
If it weren't for the hands that held her there already, I'd do it myself.
What a waste she was.
Those brown eyes, mine but not mine. Same nose, hair, ears, mouth.
Except it all looked different, and not because of the ripples across the water
caused by her panicked breathing.
No, on her, everything was hollowed out.
Inside of her, the hourglass turned, and it was made evident
by the sharp angles of her face.
The angles of her body. (When had she lost weight?)
The sand began pouring down and "Borrowed Time," a hymn of death
her bones found they liked to sing—

I lift my head from the toilet bowl.
False alarm, this time. No remnants of dinner to coat the sides
of my mouth.
Inhale, exhale.
I stand up slowly; each tentative movement feels like a concealed threat
that would send me back to the floor.
And for whatever useless reason, I decide to look in the mirror.
False alarm, this time. I don't see anything.

DRUMS AND OTHERS

Drums.
The only drums I hear are the ones inside my head.
A constant loud and unforgiving rhythm,
much like the thing in my chest that won't stop beating.
Singing.
I can't stand it; their voices rise and fall with abandon, the way mine would
within the walls of my fragile haven before I was wise enough
to trade my tongue for steel. I can only stomach a song
that sings with my heart, with whatever it's become.
The piano.
I won't be arrogant enough to say *my* piano. I have no right to call it mine.
I can't remember the last time I ran a hand along the keys and felt
gladness from it. Every touch feels like—*is*—a deception…
a half-truth at best.
Running a hand along those keys reminds me too much of where
I am—tumbling through without making a meaningful sound.
And the higher keys remind me too much of the screaming
in my head that keeps the drums company.

~~GREEN BEAR~~

Let's call him Al.
They gave him to me at the hospital.

His black eyes were beady, but not in a creepy way:
They twinkled one, two, three times,
saying they were *"Here to stay."*

FAMILY HEIRLOOM(S)

I saw the shadow of the rope swinging there. There, but not there.
The shadow moved, to hang loosely around my neck.
It almost... nuzzled against me. Rested. Like an heirloom
waiting to be passed down that was glad it finally had been.
It wanted to welcome me home
and wanted to be welcomed home in return.
But the shadow was gone as soon as it came. Why, I don't know.
I'm inclined to believe my angel could see it too.

~~HEAVY~~WEIGHT

I had chosen to place the weight of the world
on my shoulders.
It seemed too easy to put it on God's.

CHAMBER MUSIC

I tilt my head this way and that,
as if it'll ease the pounding in my skull.
I don't even have to wonder why I'm awake now.
Keeping my eyes shut and squeezing them even tighter,
I take a few moments to refamiliarize myself with my current state.
Rope—still around my wrists, the tang of their blood filling the air.
Same for my feet.
My tongue sweeps across my bottom lip—split, and more sore
than it was last time. My entire face feels more sore than last time;
I have no doubt both of my eyes are black.
Ribs, back—all bruised, I'm sure—
I stifle a hiss.
Bruises to go *with* a nasty lash across the expanse of my back.
For mouthing off.
I was in a bad mood. He told me his mood was worse.

"Turn it off."

Où est ton papa?
Dis-moi, où est ton papa?
Sans même devoir lui parler
Il sait ce qu'il ne va pas

The same song.

Où est ton papa?

I've heard it since he took me. *"Turn it off."*

The sound only grows louder. I'd prefer another beating to this.

Où est ton papa?

I want to ask him why. I want to ask Him why. I want to ask them all why, but none of them are here.

Où est ton papa?
Dis-moi, où est ton papa?
Sans même devoir lui parler
Il sait ce qu'il ne va pas

I attempt to shift my shoulders and feel the fabric of my shirt, sticky with blood from the gash in my back, shift awkwardly with the motion, the blood already mostly dried.
Should today be one of the days when I tell him to just kill me?
I've abandoned the embarrassment that begging brings.

I see movement in the darkness. One foot steps out, then the other.
Materializing from the shadows, sauntering out of them
with lethal grace.
All calculated calm and no patience, he stalks over to where I hang from the wall, footsteps more hurried than usual.
Within the span of a blink, he grips my chin and begins to tilt it up, forcing me to meet his gaze.
Wholly black eyes.

The first time he did this, however long ago that was,
I'd soiled the white dress he'd had me stuffed in.
Now, I feel nothing. Absolutely nothing.

THE MANY TALENTS OF GLASS

Did you know broken glass could cut itself too?

BLONDIE

Blonde hair, green eyes,
a wide grin that could fool everyone but me
(I'd recognize that costume anywhere).
She's got plenty of friends—
not sure how many of them are counterfeit.
A few exes who think they're owed
for something that only seemed to strike twice a day.
Head held high on low esteem,
she screams through every bout of fake laughter,
but still thinks "happily ever after" isn't just for the storybooks.
Got hooked on misfortune
as she was walking out the door of her last problem,
ninety-nine, and here's one more.
Old scars still keeping score,
doesn't even bother with long sleeves.
Her and The Past are thick as thieves,
no use in grieving blood spilled.
But the night still carries whispers on the winds
from the graves of things not quite buried.
One of them pleads, on bended knee,
"Come away with me; let's get married."
Holds out a ring made of sorrows,
"I don't wish to wait until tomorrow."

She says *no*, closes her eyes tight, and goes back to sleep.
But before she does, she looks up, begs someone above for dreams.

BEG SHOULDERS KNEES AND TOES

My wounded knees
beg, *please, tell me it isn't true.*
They've crawled for years to kiss the feet of this hard truth.
The walls of my mind were nearly painted red,
and I didn't have a clue.
How could I have lifted the bloodstain
from the carpet of a lived-in reflection?
I have another question: Were you clueless too?

SHE'S UGLY

Stop making Broken pretty.
She's one of the ugliest people I've ever met.

IT'S NOT MY PARTY AND I'LL CRY IF I WANT TO

This life thing was just a party she wasn't invited to,
and what a sad idiot she would be to beg for that invitation.
Before she did that, she'd buy herself another cake.

I THINK I KNOW

I think I know why I loved him so much.
He was the words I could still make out beneath the pen smudges.
When your brain doesn't carry many of those,
you hold onto the ones it does manage to keep,
your heart a trembling hand clutching with a white-knuckled fist.
I was lost back then in every sense of the word,
constantly wandering from place to place to find one that wasn't scary.
It was as simple as that; though the baggage was certainly complicated.
Then one day, I just decided—I'm quite sure the choice was
subconscious—that if I had to be lost, he was a good place to start.
I was right.
It didn't matter which corner of him I turned;
I would open a door to any room, and my heart would smile
a smile that wasn't forced.
I suppose that's why it stung so much when the caps flew
and the tassels moved from right to left.
My heart was confronted with itself and had to learn
how to smile on its own.

If you're wondering if I still love him, the answer's yes... and no.
Yes, I still love him, but certainly not like that anymore.
When I loved him back then, I loved him like I was drowning.
Loved everyone like I was drowning because I was.
And he was the piece of wood that drifted toward me on light waves.

Now, I love like I'm sitting on the shore,
its sands taking the shape of my limbs as the wind kisses
me and reminds me that it's a friend.
I love like I'm not afraid of the water.

FAIRYTALE

The thing about love stories is that
you never think of the ending as a frowning lullaby.
The end is always a love song—a fairytale—
with a walk down the aisle and a family built on the wings
of the tale and its magic.
But we never think of the ending as looking at him
for the last time,
when the room's about as crowded as your emotions
and he's not even paying attention.
The door swings shut, and five years go by.
And five more will probably follow.
Going until you're old and gray
and wondering but never knowing
if his heart was ever as happy as yours was
whenever he smiled a smile that was true.
You know the one, though your mind
can't paint the picture as pretty anymore.
(Memory is a dying flame,
a fragile and fickle thing between the mind's fingertips).
The one that came up at both corners and crinkled his eyes...
the one that was almost always followed by a laugh,
and the sound could've been a match
for how it lit your heart and reminded it
that light could indeed still exist.

FAIRYTALE II

We never think about the ending
where the room *isn't* crowded.
But if walls could talk,
they'd tell the two of you how they tried to warn you
to quit while you were ahead, but you didn't listen.
You'd ignore them, of course,
and instead focus on memorizing the shade of his eyes
because you know this will be the last time
you look at them from the eyes of a fallen heart.

I will never regret that it fell for him.
My heart is clumsy, and it's fallen a few times.
I can't recall the last time it was on its two feet.

CHAMPAIN PROBLEMS

He takes a sip from his flute,
he's never liked the taste of that stuff
anyway.
Catches her eyes from across the crowd of expensive fabric.
She thinks she's his habit,
but she's just time that he's passing.
She pulls him by his tie into the stall;
He pins her with his lips against the wall,
hikes up her dress until her thighs
and all of her little white lies are exposed.
It doesn't take long, maybe five minutes.
She'll never tell him that she missed it.
He kissed her everywhere except her lips,
and that's how she knows he missed it too.

But when she goes home, she worries about status,
Where are we going after practice?
Cold and callous, Daddy lowered her allowance.
Coach admires her devotion and prowess,
Girls, you should be more like her.
A tiny part of her still aches
for the way things were six months ago,
before he called it off out of the blue.
Climbs on top of *him*,
stares into *brown* eyes,
God, she wishes they were blue.

But if she was being truthful,
it didn't break her heart as much as her pride
because she's always been the first to say goodbye.

But when he goes home, he worries about bottles,
God, I wonder if Mom found them.
Hopefully, she couldn't see them past the bills.
Got offered some pills the other day at school,
but the last thing he needed was to lose his edge.
He can't hear past the echoes in his head,
hasn't seen the bastard in years,
hopes the deadbeat's finally dead at last.
He had one thing in his life he felt was finally worth wanting,
but wanting means borrowed time.
He'd die on the hill of her sigh,
but before he'd ever tempt forever,
he'd tell her goodbye.

FEIGNED AFFAIRS

She wiped him from her lips,
tried to forget the way his over-eager hands were on her hips.
His caresses were the bullets
and his bed was the crypt.
Lying in it, *"God, it's after three; I wanted to be* home *by now."*
Clothes hanging halfway off her body,
she tries to sneak out of his room on tiptoe
and a prayer to someone she hasn't talked to since the last time
she said *'I'll get home by eleven, eleven-thirty at the latest...'*

He'd called her up that morning, said,
"Come remind me why you're the greatest."
His wife was at work, kids at school.
He probably called an hour or two after he'd dropped them off.
They wouldn't be expecting him home;
he was gone for the weekend to a conference.
"Why don't you just call it off?" *This sham of a marriage,*
she'd left unspoken.
He leaned his head to the side—
gave her eyes that would be warm if she didn't know better,
and a look that said, *"Just be happy you're chosen."*

At least he'd been 'kind.' He wasn't the first time.
The first time, he didn't even ask.

She woke up every day,
thinking if she took enough shots of the past to the head,
she'd get drunk enough to not always wish she was dead.

HE WISHED IT WORKED

How unlucky am I,
you see,
that the bullets don't even want me?

THE MIND OF HISTORY

History was wise to forget, otherwise it'd have no tongue.

WHAT TIME SHOULD DO

Time flies when it should be walking.

shrugs

If I can be broken, so can the rules.

NEW OPTIONS IN THE TOY CHEST

I was all out of options, and the toys were different now,
so what was I supposed to do?
The dolls had grown jagged edges
and their houses had become
empty chambers awaiting their bullets.

THE THING ABOUT SUNSETS

They're just the sun's way of telling us that it's walking out the door,
taking its light right with it, and leaving us with
a couple of stars to fumble around with in the dark.
Sure, we have the moon, but the sun's setting and rising are the only things
we like to talk about. No one talks about the moon
unless the stars are involved; the moon's always moody
and has to make an effort to be fully present.
I feel like a night sky sometimes. The light has chosen to stick
around in a few places, but they're so far apart
that it hardly makes a difference, anyway.
The moon has a point, too: Why bother to be present when
you're forgotten while you're still in the room?

PLEASE DON'T LEAVE ME

It's not just the leaving,
it's the leaving out of the blue.
No warning,
like a car coming toward the driver's side,
and you wake up in the hospital wondering over and over
if it was your fault.
"Could I have seen it coming?"
"Was I not paying attention?"
You're looking and finding tons of details
that weren't there,
but you're holding onto them
because you need to hold onto something substantial—
some plausible reason other than *you didn't see it coming.*
It was an accident.
Neither of those are good enough.

IT'S NOT AS CUTE AS IT SOUNDS

"I wish I could feel nothing." No, you don't.
Try not to get in the habit of saying things you don't mean.

SLEEPY NOT SLEEPY

My bones want to go to sleep. Ever felt like that?
When you're so tired and you close your eyes for a few hours at night, then
wake up... and somehow
you're both lighter and heavier in the morning.
I think it's the scale refusing to tip in my soul's favor.
I think it's dreams dying; it must be the feeling
of carrying their bodies on my shoulders.

CLEAN UP TIME

Glass shards drape across the ground's shoulders
like a pitiful blanket.
I may have gotten a little carried away.
Everyone's entitled to a bad day.
It was all just so... clean. And neat. So pretty.
The perfection was grating my nerves. I needed at least one thing
in this house to look like me. And I'd already finished my drink, so...
I've just been standing here, staring at one of the now two imperfect things
within these walls. I should probably move before someone finds me,
but I needed a minute with someone else who understood.
A door just closed. I should clean this up now.

DRUG OF CHOICE

PRESENT
We weren't best friends, despite what it looked like. We didn't even like each other that much, and we certainly weren't good for each other in any capacity. Whenever we hung out, it was kind of like...
Think of that first drink of cold water, when you can feel it going all the way down, and after about three seconds, the sensation's gone.

PAST
For three seconds, I am absolutely, inexplicably alive.
For the other 86, 397 seconds in the day, I'm—
Not dead because I'm still breathing.
Not alive because I'm only breathing.
Just breathing. Nothing else. Inhale, exhale. Inhale, exhale.

Inhale
(I give nothing),
exhale
 (but I'm trying to).

PRESENT
Our involvement with each other lasted longer than it should've.

SACRIFICE

None of it counted unless I ripped myself open,
spilled onto the stone of the altar,
bled down the sides of it,
and pooled around the feet of those around me.

SAVIOR

You would've thought I could heal and raise the dead:
I had this way of placing sins on myself like no other.
Like when they got drunk,
I always thought of myself as one of the sorrows
they'd try to drown with the liquor on their lips—
because if I could be a sorrow,
then I could be a salvation.

~~If I was better, maybe they wouldn't have~~
~~felt the need to choose the pills today.~~
~~If I was better, maybe they wouldn't have wound up~~
~~in the wrong bed,~~
~~with who they thought was the right person~~
~~until they woke up.~~
~~If I'd done this, that, and the other~~
~~to prevent all the things~~
~~that had nothing to do with me,~~
~~then maybe they wouldn't have happened~~
~~and everybody would be happier...~~
~~And I wouldn't feel so terrible for dropping the world~~
~~because its weight was too heavy on my shoulders.~~

IF ONLY

If only somebody had told me,
it would've saved me
from the many forsaken soliloquies
that soaked the sheets of my bed
and nearly drowned
the night curtains at the window.
I'm up to my knees in words
I don't say to anybody but me.

EMPTY ~~BOTTLES~~

At the bottom, I'll find second chances.
There's an X that marks the spot
of a love that's not demanded.
There's vengeance for the innocence stolen—
made off like a bandit.
There's a hope that, for once,
my hands won't feel so empty-handed.

She swears by the glasses like an oath,
she picks the petals of Unsettled,
roams the field where it grows.

JAILBIRD

I'm held hostage by words that never left their mouths.
I'm behind the bars of the looks on their faces.

STROBE LIGHTS

I'm at the party.
I'm in mourning, but no one knows because by the morning,
I'm 'fine.'
"Just tired." My well-loved lie.

I've been crying since July of last year... or maybe June or May.
Faces crowded around the table, laughing at all the jokes told
by Yesterday.
(When's the last time I ate today?)
I don't hear a single word they say. The lights are flashing,
blue red green.
Blue for the black, that's the bruise of losing him,
red for the bloodshed of never saying goodbye,
green for the night he drove out the city and never told me *why*.
(Did he love me?
Was it a figment of my desperate imagination?
Did he love me?
Was it Fear that lost its balance and bumped into Manipulation,
got the stain of it on its clothes? A ruse that was scared
and purely accidental?
Because your eyes were too sweet to ever hurt me on purpose.)
Whatever it was, broken is as broken does, I hope it was worth it.

I'm at the party.
I'm in mourning, but no one knows because by the morning,
I'm 'fine.'

MIDAS

~~I wish you weren't a weaker man.~~
~~Most beggars don't choose, yet somehow you can.~~
~~Born with a mouth known to bite the hand that feeds you.~~

Bent shoulders, bottles, drugs.
I don't want to ask about the way it was.
Full on spirits, empty love.
The curse was never in your words; it was always in the touch.
Despite your pride's lies, your hands didn't leave gold.
They left dreams and desires,
arms wrapped around their knees
in the cold of where you left the kid who looks just like you.
Left the one thing in your life that somehow remained true.

There's hell in the 'had been,' hell in the habits,
 ice in the six-feet-under casket.

BABY'S BLUE

Little Miss Mary was seen as quite contrary
when she wouldn't let his eager hands unbutton her blouse.
He ran out of the house and went to tell
the whole town what he had found.
"There's a girl around the corner,
as beautiful as can be,
but there's another—easy lover, never going to meet your mother,
probably just rolled out of your brother's bed the night before—
she's right down the street.
Not as pretty as Mary.
Hanging on by a thread, just barely.
A darkness in her eyes,
could be ghosts or the weight of a world she carries.
But she's not seeking a savior or a doting, devoted spouse.
She's looking for hands that aren't looking for answers,
just for what she's wearing
beneath the flimsy fabric of her baby blue blouse."

IF I WERE HONEST FOR A SECOND, ~~BUT I RAN OUT OF TIME~~

I would ask them one by one why I was only ever good enough
to be a death-bed regret.
I would ask, if the skies were always clear, and
"You always treated us best,"
why the age-old myth of never loving me was never laid to rest.

Questions on questions and for once,
I've never cared about answers.
I've been battered, disturbed, and beaten
by your sadistic reasons,
tried and convicted for Time's treason.

INSECURITIES

I don't really think I'm pretty,
and I think anyone who says it is lying to me,
trying to spare what's left of my bereft and barren feelings.
I think my smile is too animated,
the corners relatively past the corner of Elated,
walking down the street of What Is She So Happy About?
So, whenever we go out, I leave my real smile at the house.
I think my eyes are too dreamlike for a boy to fall in love with;
perhaps he thinks they'd be too easy to get lost in,
in a way that's unromantic.
I can't be imagining the suppressed panic behind all their eyes
when they look into mine.
Alice, stop your wondering.
I can't come into this wandering land of your sparkling imagination.
It ends before it begins.
I close my eyes and live with the Hatter who's mad
and all of my friends.

STOP CALLING ME THAT

Always called me golden,
but I think he just mistook me for something that glittered.

IT'S NOT SPIDERS

My biggest fear...
waking one day and finding I've been a person's chains.
It's an ever-present current
beneath the surface of my thoughts, every one.
The blood in the veins of them, truly.
I would hate to be a cage.

SUNNY

Once there was a boy named Sunny,
who found most—if not *all* things—quite funny.
He smiled and smiled his noons and nights away,
like both would always be there to stay.
His lover was the setting of him;
her grins and laughter were not so easily given.
The town would tell him over and over,
"We believe you've made a grave mistake, Sunny,"
but he would always tell them back,
"She's the reason I'm risen."
One day, the green-eyed shrew,
eyes sharp as talons, as a cunning tongue,
lost her nerve—
in her hands, she found a weapon to bring the rains.
And Sunny, the foolishly trusting,
his back was turned to her wicked ways.

In one blink, bound.
In another, blood drawn.
In three, the skies darkened and the light had fallen.

~~~~~

Daisies, daisies, daisies.
They grow all around the stones.
It has been many years since the light has shone.
And every year, to the day,
she walks among the stones to find one and say,
"The day I met you, I curse the day."

CUT MYSELF "SHAVING"

People always talk about
picking yourself up, as if it's some easy thing;
as if you're not cutting yourself
on your own jagged edges as you try to do so.

GALLOWS

The gallows are down the road,
I can see them from my window.
Their whispers carry down the dirt path.
They say,
"We've never met a man we couldn't hold
as close as he held the sins of his father."
I hear at the end of their whispers that it's time to come home.

~~UN~~NATURAL DISASTERS

Humans are a lot like houses, you know?
It takes only one natural disaster to flood our memories,
crack the floors of us to the very foundations,
soak us to the bone.
And you say it's natural until it's you.

PILL POPPER

One of my favorite hobbies is popping pills,
but don't worry; they're just the ones that are hard to swallow.

COLD WATER

Sometimes you have to sit in the disappointment,
like sitting in a tub until the water runs cold.

SHE HAD YOUR BABY

So you came back.
"Hey."
"How've you been?"
Waited a couple conversations
till you told me you got her pregnant.
Saw the pictures; the kid looks just like you.
Had to pretend each one wasn't a fist
that made my heart more black and blue than it already was.
I guess we grew up,
but my dreams were still young,
and they hung onto stolen gazes
and silly faces made across the room just to make each other laugh.
If a picture's worth a thousand words,
how many are in a memory of the past?
I don't think there's a limit,
but when one speaks to me, I listen.
And right now it sounds like it's telling me, "I told you so."

AND I DIDN'T EVEN NEED ADVERTISING

The folks are buying what I'm selling
'cause what I'm selling is myself short.
Suffice it to say, the price they pay
is one they can easily afford
because the shots are cheap, the blows are low.
How small the cost for what was lost
and for what I keep on losing.
But if I'm the only one who sees the black and blue,
does it still count as bruising?
Or is it all fun and games
until I no longer look the same
and don't even recognize my own reflection?
Now that you mention it,
when was the last time I saw her?

WHAT I LEARNED TO DO WITH FEELINGS

Bottle them up like wine and indulge later.
(I lied and told myself they'd taste better with age.)

A FUN FACT ABOUT THE DEVIL

The devil's not always this loud, growling thing,
and I wish I'd known that when I was younger.

More often than not, he isn't obvious—
he's more like the trail of smoke
that slips in through the cracks,
or the noise you hear when you try to convince yourself
it's just the wind.
He's the chill that raises the hairs on the back of your neck
and you wonder where it came from
because the day is warm,
the sky is blue—not a cloud to be seen.

I sat there in the front row, hand on his arm (small thing it was)
as he motioned for the curtains to be lifted,
and that's what I remember most.
The play itself—I easily confuse the details:
who said what where, who did what at what point in the story.
But I remember the wave of his hand
because it looked like he'd done it a thousand times.
Such arrogance... and I wondered how many other girls
in pretty white dresses had been forced to sit here in this spot
before me, before he was through with them, too.

KIDDIE DRAWINGS

Accomplishments, nah, but failures?
Hung 'em and stared like they were bad drawings on a fridge.

MIDNIGHT

It's midnight.
I think he's off getting high.

He's off getting high on the low rise of her old jeans,
fingers running along the seams
like they've got somewhere to be.
He's eager; she is, too.
Walking backwards into his bedroom.
They've fallen onto the sheets.
Pushes me out of his mind until it's over.
Rolls over, kisses her shoulder.

Rolls back into town, reads the upside down smile
in my eyes from across the room, strolls over.
Taps my shoulder, *Let me explain.*
Tried to tell me all the ways it wasn't personal,
as if her body on his wasn't a vendetta.
Was he expecting a welcome as warm
as his arm draped across her hip?
Read the farewell kiss of my lips: *I'm through.*

~~~~~

It's midnight.
She's probably already wasted.

His hand kissed her face and left a lipstick stain.
Then she held her breath and went beneath
the rivers of the shame she wanted to die from,
lungs beginning to fill and burn with regret
because how many times had his empty promises
burned her like a cigarette?

~~~~~

It's midnight.
I think he's off getting high, and she's probably already wasted.

A SAD GIRL MOMENT

Before you go, can you at least tell me what it is
that makes you all come to the same conclusion?
Warn me, so next time I can avoid unnecessary bruises.
Am I too much or am I too little?
Or are both of those one and the same?
This is one of those moments when I wonder
what it would be like if I had another's name.
The name of a girl who wouldn't be the game
no one wanted to play.

TIED UP

Everything's always tied up with me when it comes to him.
Hands, tongue, whatever.

Maybe it's the way all of the words are about him,
even when they aren't,
all tied to him by this invisible, intangible part of me
that chooses to love him quiet, chooses to love him loud.
Hand around my heart's mouth,
you can still make out the words
that I will love him for all eternity.

TIED UP II

It's one of those things I learned
that doesn't really feel like learning, more like milestones—
like tying your shoes or riding a bike.
I learned to love him like that.
Tighten the knot of him on me whenever loving him gets loose
because these days it does, often.
So I tie it twice around for good measure,
like it'll make a difference.

MATH

2+2 is 4, yet somehow we got 5.
6, 7, 8, where were you on the 9th?
Ten toes down, standing on bad business.

Whose open thighs were your lies between?
Tell me where you were on the 13th.
On second thought, forget about it.
You'll just pretend none of it counts
and try to go back to normal.
"Just like we used to."
That's over now, trying to back out of the room
of lies that were never white—
it's become so crowded, and I can hardly see
behind the clouds in my eyes, anyway.
I won't beg for you to stay, this time.

I've got somewhere to be on the 29th.

Acknowledgements

Always God, first and foremost. (Even though You gave me a brain that mostly likes to write when I'm actively trying to do other things like take naps lol.)
Once again, thank you Reyna for the art on this cover. I don't think anyone else's art can quite 'get me' like yours does, and in case you weren't already aware you're stuck with me forever.
Kathryn Palmer, my magical editing queen.
M.A. Rehman, coolest cover designer ever.
Family and friendssssss—I always feel *all* the love and support you constantly give me, and I wish I could articulate it better with actual words, but unfortunately God only made me good with a pen, so I guess this will have to do. I love you <3.
Reader... I hope this finds you well (ik that sounds very cliché, but it's true). I hope in this book, at the very least, you found a kindred spirit.

About the Author

God, how do people write these things?
Last time, I opted for my default setting of sarcasm, but this time around I'm coming up empty.
Hm. I'll state a few random facts and get out of your way, I suppose? *Ahem*:

1. I honestly do not know why I was born in the South. I love cardigans too much.
2. I'm not really fond of things that fly. (Namely birds, birds are evil... okayyyy, maybe not evil, but my body starts to lose feeling whenever one is closer than 15 feet, so they're still not that great.)
3. I wish my natural hair color was red—not normal *orange* red, Bryce Quinlan red.
4. I probably consume entirely too much peanut butter.
5. I am, quite frankly, very tired of the overrated praise that fruit receives on a consistent basis. It's *bleh* at best, and there are maybe only three or four that you can actually enjoy *on their own,* without the assistance of covering them in chocolate or some other sweet dip that tries to disguise the pure blandness of the actual fruit itself.

That's all. If you happen to agree with me about the fruit thing, or about anything else, or if you just so happen to enjoy my writing outside of my pitiful *About the Author* attempts, follow me on IG: @joyyy_reads. <33

Copyright ©2025 Joyah Aleyxsis Claiborne, Aleyxsis Publishing
All rights reserved. No part of this book may be reproduced, stored, or transmitted in any form by any means—electronic, mechanical, photocopy, recording, or otherwise—without the express written permission of the publisher.